A Gathering Of Angels
Inspired Writings
By
Sandra J Yearman

Seraphim Publishing LLC

WE WILL BRING LIGHT TO ALL THE DARK PLACES

Registered trademark-Sandra J Yearman
Seraphim Publishing
438 Water St
Cambridge, WI 53523

Copyright © 2008 Sandra J Yearman
Produced in the United States of America
Author : Sandra J Yearman
Editor: Sandra J Yearman
Cover Design by Sandra J Yearman
Layout and design by Sandra J Yearman

All rights reserved. No part of this book may be reproduced, stored in or introduced into a retrieval system, or transmitted, in any form or by any means, electronic or mechanical, including photocopying or recording or otherwise copied for public or private use—other than for "fair use" as brief quotations embodied in articles and reviews--without written permission from the author.

Library of Congress Control Number: 2009900439
ISBN: 978-0-9815791-0-8
First Edition

They Gathered In The Darkness
To Save God's Children There
To Protect Them From Their Choices
To Ease The Burdens That They Bear
Amen
Amen
Amen

CONTENTS

DEDICATION

A Gathering Of Angels............................7
Praise..8
God Look Upon....................................10
Angels Gathered...................................12
The Cross And The Sword......................14
A Little Angel......................................16
Angel And Dove....................................18
Gabriel...21
Thank You God, For Angels....................22
Ask Them To Stay.................................24
The Scales And The Sword.....................26
Angels In Their Glory............................28
I Have A Friend In Heaven.....................30
Bless Them With God's Song..................32

SEEKING LIGHT IN THE DARKNESS

Who Do They Serve...............................35
Vacant Eyes..37
Death...39

CONTENTS

The Roar They Never Heard......................40
Why Do We Harm Ourselves...................43
Truth..45
He Always Held My Hand..........................47
Rising From The Ashes................................49
God's Song..51
Question Through The Ages......................52
I Am Choking..54
A Walk Through Horror.............................55
Little Child..58
Battlefield Of Old.......................................60

COMING HOME

You Said..64
Throughout All Ends..................................66
Transcend..68
If You Call My Name..................................70
Christ Our Savior..72
They Gathered In The Darkness................73

Dedication

Gathering Of Angels

A gathering of Angels
In Holy union sing
The praises of the Lord
Their Father and their King

A gathering of Angels
Herald the Father's Name
Send blessings to His children
Send tidings of the same

A gathering of Angels
In Holy unison
Celebrate in Heaven
The Victory is won

Amen Amen Amen

Praise

Praise to the Father
Praise to the Son
Praise to the Spirit
The Holy One

Praise to all Heaven
For Mercy and Grace
Praise to the Angels
Who darkness do face

Pray that creation
The work of God's Hand
Will gather its faith
And darkness withstand

Pray that the child
Who God loves so much
Sings to the Lord
For His Holy touch

And pray that all Angels
Who gather this night
Will bless us and save us
With God's Holy Might

Amen Amen Amen

God Look Upon

God look upon this Holy family
Fill us with Your Grace
Consume us with Your Presence
Save us in this place

Protect us from the darkness
No matter what form it takes
Walk with us always
Let us not be filled with fear and hate

Smile upon this family
Bless our every task
Protect us from all horror
Expose the demon masks

And when our time here has ended
Return us to our Home
In the arms of an Angel
In darkness no more to roam

Amen Amen Amen

Angels Gathered

The Angels gathered to sing God's
praises
The Great All
The Majesty of Heaven

The Angels gathered to dance
The stars of Heaven exploded with
light
And the Son of God was sent to rescue
A world dying in darkness

The Angels gathered to rejoice
The world took notice
Messengers from God filled
the darkness
A promise of God was fulfilled

The world was blessed
The world was rescued
The world was redeemed

Lord God, we love You
Thank You for our blessings
Thank You for our gifts
Thank You for the miracles

Amen Amen Amen

The Cross And The Sword

He showed us with His actions
He taught us with His words
That the mightiest of warriors
The cross and sword do gird

David conquered many
And surrendered to His King
Jesus conquered all
And Salvation did bring

Moses saved a nation
David united the worlds
Jesus saved us through all times
The cross and sword do gird

Many desire power
Regardless of the form
But faith is the strongest power
To conquer all the storms

And the Holiest of warriors
On bended knees did pray
To our Holy Father in Heaven
To turn darkness into day

Amen Amen Amen

A Little Angel

A little Angel was sent to earth
To prepare the Holy Way
To open the hearts of people
For the most glorious of days

This little Angel taught God's children
Who had forgotten the Holy Ways
That the Lord is always with us
Until the end of days

She sang the Songs of Heaven
She brought the Spirit in
To the most forgotten creatures
To help redeem them from their sin

She sang the praises
Of the most ancient of Kings
And she reminded the world of Angels
The Holy Songs did ring

A path she lit in the darkness
The words she taught of the Song
She blessed a world of darkness
And asked God to heal the wrongs

The little Angel, she created
Lights to show the Way
So sheep could find the Shepherd
Until night turned into day

Amen Amen Amen

Angel And Dove

I saw an Angel
In a dream
Holding a dove
Lord what does this mean

The message escaped me
What did I not see
Was this merely a dream
Or a message from Thee

A second night
I had the same dream
The image was real
Or so it seemed

I pondered
What can this be
Is it merely a dream
Or a message from Thee

The third night
I saw her again
An Angel, a dove
Holiness reign

This night
She spoke to me
'This is more than a dream'
'This is a message to help you see'

'God speaks to you'
'In many ways'
'He speaks to everyone'
'All their days'

'But the messages'
'Are not always recognized'
'People do not believe'
'What is before their eyes'

'God sends His blessings'
'God sends His Love'
'Be open to messages'
'Sent from above'

Amen Amen Amen

Gabriel

He stood before His Presence
He was a messenger of His birth
His name is known in Heaven
His name is known on earth

An Angel in his Glory
Has visited us many times
To teach us the Word of God
To show us the Holy signs

Gabriel brought His message
Gabriel announced the King
Gabriel showed the Way
And the Miracles we sing

Amen Amen Amen

Thank You God, For Angels

Angels send good tidings
To the worlds below
Love and Grace
In their Holiness bestow

Angels pray for God's children
And watch them where they go
They ask the Lord to keep them
In their Holiness bestow

Angels guard us always
Although their presence is unknown
They ask the Lord to save us
In their Holiness bestow

God thank You for the Angels
That guard us, though unseen
May we feel their Holy presence
May we understand their meaning

Amen Amen Amen

Ask Them To Stay

Angels in their Glory
Are filled with delight
When God's children
Seek them in the night

When we choose to listen
When we choose to pray
When we seek them out
And ask them to stay

With us forever
Hold our hands that we
May feel their Heavenly Presence
May experience the Love of Thee

Angels in their Glory
Send us Love each day
And ask that we do listen
And not to turn them away

Amen Amen Amen

The Scales And The Sword

God sent him down for Justice
He carried the Scales and Sword
To teach us of Mercy
To teach us of the Lord

For Holiness to balance
The Scales and the Sword
Can only be understood
If you love like the Lord

Michael fought the darkness
The beasts he cast away
He showed us with his actions
That they could be conquered in this way

He is an Angel Warrior
Mercy is his vest
He moves with the Grace of God
He conquered all the tests

He taught us with his actions
He taught us of the Lord
The Archangel
Who carries the Scales and the Sword

Amen Amen Amen

Angels In Their Glory

All the orders of Angels
Represent God's Love
The Holy messengers
The guardians from above

Each and every order
Signifies and stands
For Love, Justice and Holiness
God holds us in His Hands

Angels in their Glory
Numbers three by three
Witness through the ages
The lives of man they see

Each and every Angel
A creation unique
Pray to the Heavens
Their presence to seek

Amen Amen Amen

I Have A Friend In Heaven

I have a friend in Heaven
A light so bright as to blind
I call her my guardian Angel
I always ask to see a sign

I know she watches over
For I have been richly blessed
I have been saved many times
While taking this earthly test

I have seen her in my memory
I have seen her in my dreams
She has come to me in darkness
When she has heard my screams

Her presence makes me wonder
To seek what I can not see
Lord, have You sent me a friend from Heaven
A gift to watch over me

Amen Amen Amen

Bless Them With God's Song

This world is always in crisis
People filled with anger and pain
No matter where you look
The hands of man are stained

I have often wondered
How do you take a stand
How do you stop the darkness
In this world of man

No matter how I studied
No matter how I prayed
The answers to my questions
Eluded me many days

Then my eyes were opened
The answers were before me all along
To destroy the darkness
Bless it with God's Song

Amen Amen Amen

Seeking Light In The Darkness

Who Do They Serve

The battle rages
A warrior dies
God welcomes him
He transcends the skies

The armies move
To songs of old
Battles for power
Land and gold

What song do they march to
To whom do they serve
What allegiances do they honor
What honors do they deserve

Battlefields
Are drawn in the sand
Is this our glory
Is this the destiny of man

What is our focus
What is our take
God help us to understand our role
For all creations sake

Amen Amen Amen

Vacant Eyes

Vacant eyes
Hollow stares
People of the worlds
Do we really care

Their faces are everywhere
The hunger, the depression, the despair
We see them in the media
The vacant eyes and hollow stares

Their faces haunt us
They make us cry
Do we seek to help them
Or just wonder why

We are all God's children
Every color and creed
How are we judged
What is our need

Do we take time to listen
Do we make time to care
For the children of God
Are everywhere

Amen Amen Amen

Death

I have seen death at my door step
I have seen death in this place
I have seen death devour
I have seen death erase

Death can be conquered
Death can be fought
For all God's children
Salvation was bought

With the Blood of the Holy
With the Promise of a King
Through the Love of God
And the Blessings that brings

Amen Amen Amen

The Roar They Never Heard

The lightening thundered loudly
The clouds tore through the storm
The armies marched in silence
Their spirits wet and worn

The fighting goes forever
Man's role to most is lost
The armies never ending
The victories forever sought

They marched into the darkness
Blinded by hatred and greed
They followed a dark knight
Who had many hellacious needs

They came upon a village
Aglow with Holy light
This small village
Stood out in the darkness of the night

The madness of the dark knight
Drove him to many sins
The people of the village
Were unaware of the danger
they were in

God watched as the armies of darkness
Marched across the barren land
Now that they endangered
His children
He took a Holy stand

The earth shook with thunder
The roar they never heard
As the ground opened up
As the waters were disturbed

The dark knight and his demons
Were swept back into hell
The village peacefully slept
The villagers peacefully dwelled

God protects us always
Even when we are unaware
Because He is our Father
Because He always cares

Amen Amen Amen

Why Do We Harm Ourselves

God gave you a gift
A precious gift of life
A perfect vessel
A testament that God loves you

And you said to God
This gift is imperfect
This gift does not please me
I want to destroy this gift

You allow darkness and despair to overtake you
You disfigure this gift
You torture this gift
You kill this gift

Lord, help us to learn to love and accept ourselves as the precious gifts You created

Lord, help us to remember the Holiness in all of Your creations

Lord, please save us from ourselves

Amen Amen Amen

Truth

Man desires freedom
The ages do not change
We die, we kill for freedom
Our lives we would arrange

Freedom comes in many forms
And in many degrees
But the only true freedom
Is sent from the most Holy

Truth brings Light to the darkness
Truth can topple walls
Truth can transcend us
Truth can give us All

Truth will give us freedom
From the illusions we live in
Truth will remind us
How to return to where we begin

Amen Amen Amen

He Always Held My Hand

I have traveled greatly
Searching for a song
Looking for a meaning
Questioning right and wrong

I have taken the wrong road
And gotten lost many times
I always cry to Heaven
And ask to be shown a sign

Some times it comes in whispers
Some times it comes with a roar
Some times I barely notice
Some times I can not ignore

For when I call to Heaven
I always get a sign
I always find an answer
Sent from the Divine

It may not be in the package
I asked for
It may not be in a form I recognize
But I trust it is the perfect answer
Because God is perfect, God is wise

Now as my days do number
And I dwell upon my life
I see I was sent an answer
When ever I was filled with strife

For God was always with me
Even when I feared that I was lost
He always held my hand
And gave me the answers that I sought

Amen Amen Amen

Rising From The Ashes

Rising from the ashes
As the worlds fall away
Are we made of Spirit
Are we made of clay

Rising from the ashes
Christ has shown us the Way
To have that life of Spirit
To leave the worlds of clay

Rising from the ashes
He showed us with His life
We can transcend the darkness
We can choose to leave this strife

Rising from the ashes
Is a Holy test
Conquering the darkness
Living with the blessed

Amen Amen Amen

God's Song

I was told that I was dying
The doctors took the tests
They said they would do surgery
They said they would try their best

When the shock was over
I prayed upon my knees
'God let Your will be done'
'To You I will release'

Some say it was a miracle
I say it was God's Song
I am whole and I am healthy
God corrected what was wrong

Amen Amen Amen

Question Through The Ages

Is hell the same for every one
A question asked of old
Do we determine our destinies
Do we determine what we have sold

Are we in control of our lives here
Are we in control of the tests
Do we determine the choices
Are we truly blessed

Is there a God in Heaven
Do Angels walk among
What are the consequences of
our actions
The ancient songs are sung

These questions have been asked
through the ages
By men of many worlds
By wise men and by sages
The questions they do swirl

The answers are before us
God whispers in the wind
Ask to hear His Voice
Ask to take His Wisdom in

Amen Amen Amen

I Am Choking

God I am choking on the deeds I have done
On the sins I have committed

God I am dying
I have killed myself
Your Holy creation
My darkness already decays

Please forgive me
Please lift me out of this hell I have created
Please save me

God please breathe Your Holy Spirit into me
God I choose life
God I choose You

Amen Amen Amen

A Walk Through Horror

They gasped with horror
As they were led
Through the remains of a place
Where the demons stored their dead

God look upon Your children
Bless us with Your Grace
Send Your Angels to protect us
From the horror of this place

The watchers wept
Tears of compassion and pain
At the cruelty of humanity
At what cost, at what gain

God look upon Your children
Bless us with Your Grace
Send Your Angels to protect us
From the horror of this place

Cruelty beyond comprehension
Hatred with disgrace
A monument to demons
A God forsaken place

God look upon Your children
Bless us with Your Grace
Send Your Angels to protect us
From the horror of this place

Lord, let not the world of man
Relive such horror and pain
Let us not give power to the demons
Let history no longer be stained

God look upon Your children
Bless us with Your Grace
Send Your Angels to protect us
From the horror of this place

With the blood of innocents
Saturating our souls and hands
Let us not give power to the demons
In this world of man

God look upon Your children
Bless us with Your Grace
Send Your Angels to protect us
From the horror of this place

Instead let You walk among us
Let Your Presence fill every place
Save us from ourselves
Bless us with Your Grace

Amen Amen Amen

Little Child

Little child do not fear
There are no monsters in the night
The Lord is always watching
And protecting you with His Might

Little child go to Him
And say what is in your heart
For He is your Holy Father
For from you He will never be apart

Little child sleep safely
Know that Angels watch over you
God hears all your prayers
God sees all that you do

Little child walk with God
And know that He is Love
That He will always help you
And watch you from above

Amen Amen Amen

Battlefield Of Old

The armies of darkness gathered
On a battle field of old
To fight for the power
To steal creation's souls

The monsters fought each other
Their hatred and their rage
The battle was so bloody
Set on death's horrid stage

The demons fought for power
The demons fought for control
The demons killed each other
To steal creation's souls

And from the mist a voice cried
So faint and so weak
'God save us from our darkness'
'Your Holiness to seek'

The voice cried for creation
The voice cried to save their souls
The voice cried up to the Heavens
And stirred within God's Soul

And God in His Mercy
Answers all our prayers
He heard the little Angel
Who fought the darkness there

For in her imperfection
She ran ahead the rest
To try and save creation
To past the Holy test

And God in His Mercy
Sent His Angels down
For the cry of even one voice
To Heaven will astound

God listens to our voices
God answers all our prayers
God loves it when we call to Him
And ask Him to join us there

Amen Amen Amen

Coming Home

You Said

You said I would always be protected
If I believed in Your Grace
If I called out to the Heavens
If I walked with You in this place

You said You would hold me
When I was about to fall
You said all I had to do
Was to believe You are the All

You said that You would shelter me
Through the darkness of my days
Even when I denied You
Even when I went a stray

You said that You would test us
You said You would forgive
You said we have the choice
To die or to live

And true You are to Your Word
And truly are the tests
And through Your Son Jesus
We have been eternally Blessed

Amen Amen Amen

Throughout All Ends

They write about Awakening
They write about the Trail of Tears
But overcoming darkness
Is overcoming our fears

God has sent us many teachers
Who have shown us with their lives
We do not merely read the words
But with actions we do strive

But the theme that has the center
In all the stories told
Is a theme most Holy
Since the days of old

Faith in what He teaches
Faith in what He sends
Faith in His Love
Faith throughout all ends

Amen Amen Amen

Transcend

As the battle rages
The time of Angels is at hand
For the Holy Spirit
To fill this world of man

To awaken us from our nightmares
To remind us of our Home
To help us find our Way back
From Heaven no more to roam

To conquer the illusions
That we have created to separate
To help us conquer darkness
To show us the Holy Gate

To teach us how to transcend
The boundaries of time and space
To surpass the frailties of humanity
To Bless us with God's Grace

Amen Amen Amen

If You Call My Name

You will not take this journey alone,
God said
If you choose to travel in the Light
I will send you a Lamp
To Light your Way in the night

I will be with you always
If you choose to call out My Name
I will send you a Shepherd
Who will carry you when you are lame

I will carry you always
If you love Me like my child
I will send Angels to guide you
In these worlds, all your whiles

I will Love you always
Said the Father to the Son
Your sins have been forgiven
Through Jesus Christ, the Holy One

Amen Amen Amen

Christ Our Savior

Christ our Savior
Heavenly King
Angels honor
Heaven sings

Walk among us
Angel, man
Carry our hearts
Carry us in Your Hands

Bring us Light
Peace and Grace
Bless us with Love
In Your Name sake

Amen Amen Amen

They Gathered In The Darkness

They gathered in the darkness
To save God's children there
To protect them from their choices
To ease the burdens that they bear

They engulf us with their presence
They engulf us with their Grace
But God's children
Do not recognize their face

Ask to see the face of Angels
Ask to hear their voices sing
Ask to feel their presence near you
And the Love that they do bring

Ask God to give you Holy Sight
To help you understand
There is much more to our existence
Than the world of man

Amen Amen Amen

As The Battle Rages
The Time Of Angels Is At Hand
For The Holy Spirit
To Fill This World Of Man
Amen
Amen
Amen

www.ingramcontent.com/pod-product-compliance
Lightning Source LLC
Chambersburg PA
CBHW051714040426
42446CB00008B/874